SEASON'S GREETINGS

Season's Greetings

A Hatched and Patched Christmas

Anni Downs

Season's Greetings: A Hatched and Patched Christmas
© 2015 by Anni Downs

Martingale®
19021 120th Ave. NE, Ste. 102
Bothell, WA 98011-9511 USA
ShopMartingale.com

Printed in China
20 19 18 17 16 15   8 7 6 5 4 3 2 1

**Library of Congress Cataloging-in-Publication Data
is available upon request.**

ISBN: 978-1-60468-718-7

MISSION STATEMENT

Dedicated to providing quality products and service
to inspire creativity.

CREDITS

PUBLISHER AND CHIEF VISIONARY OFFICER
Jennifer Erbe Keltner

EDITORIAL DIRECTOR
Karen Costello Soltys

DESIGN DIRECTOR
Paula Schlosser

ACQUISITIONS EDITOR
Karen M. Burns

PHOTOGRAPHER
Brent Kane

TECHNICAL EDITOR
Mary V. Green

PRODUCTION MANAGER
Regina Girard

COPY EDITOR
Marcy Heffernan

ILLUSTRATOR
Rose Wright

CONTENTS

INTRODUCTION

When I was growing up, Christmas was always about family. Every Christmas morning we would wake up far too early, investigate our Santa bags, then make a two-hour trip to Sydney to see the extended family—cousins galore! It was always so much fun. We'd all congregate around the Christmas tree, play, talk, explore everyone's new toy stash, and eat too much, with the Christmas pudding being the highlight at lunch.

It's only now that I have my own family I realize how much work goes on behind the scenes to make everything so special, so I'd like to dedicate this book to my mother, father, aunts, uncles, and grandparents, for making the effort to produce The Ultimate Christmas every year.

Have fun,
Anni

GENERAL INSTRUCTIONS

In these projects, you'll find hand embroidery, but also appliqué, piecing, and a little hand quilting. Read this section first to learn how to use the patterns in the book as well as other useful information.

You can find additional helpful information on quilting at ShopMartingale.com/HowtoQuilt.

BEFORE YOU BEGIN

- Read all instructions carefully.
- Use ¼" seam allowances. Seam allowances are included in the cutting sizes given unless otherwise indicated.
- Sew all fabric pieces with right sides together unless otherwise stated.
- Press all seam allowances toward darker fabric or in the direction that creates the least bulk.
- Refer to photos and diagrams for color placement and block orientation.
- All yardage requirements are based on 42"-wide fabric unless otherwise noted and are given at the beginning of each project. The fabric requirements given are for non-directional fabrics only.
- "Pattern sheet 1" and "pattern sheet 2" refer to the pullout sheets at the back of the book.

SUPPLIES

I used DMC cotton floss for all the projects in this book. The colors I used are listed below, but the colors you use should be determined by the fabrics you choose. (For a project-by-project list of colors, go to ShopMartingale.com/Extras.) Use two strands from the six-strand embroidery floss unless otherwise stated.

- Blue (DMC 3768)
- Brown (DMC 610)
- Caramel (DMC 422)
- Cream (DMC 3047)
- Dark coffee (DMC 167)
- Dark taupe (DMC 3021)
- Dusky rose (DMC 356)
- Ecru (DMC Ecru)
- Gray (DMC 924)
- Green (DMC 580)
- Light brown (DMC 612)
- Medium teal (DMC 502)
- Mustard (DMC 782)
- Orange (DMC 921)
- Red (DMC 221)
- White (DMC Blanc)
- Yellow (DMC 3852)

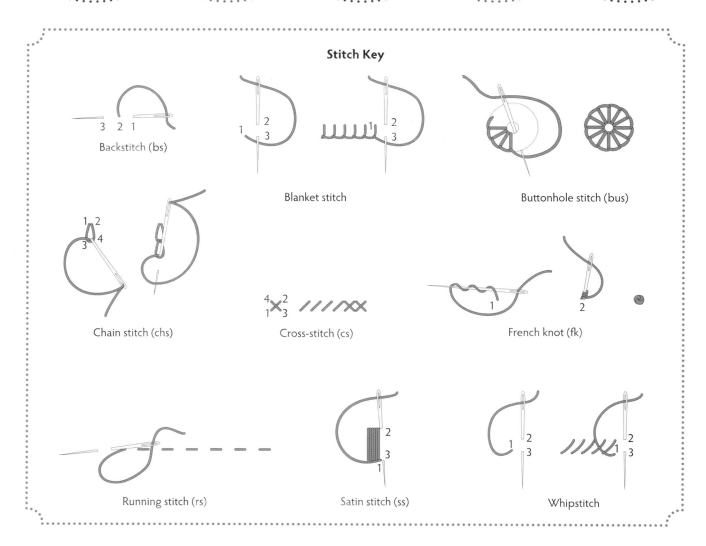

Stitch Key

Backstitch (bs)

Blanket stitch

Buttonhole stitch (bus)

Chain stitch (chs)

Cross-stitch (cs)

French knot (fk)

Running stitch (rs)

Satin stitch (ss)

Whipstitch

You'll also need a pencil, a water-soluble marker, heat-resistant template plastic, freezer paper (optional; this depends on your preferred appliqué technique), a brown Pigma pen, and general sewing supplies.

APPLIQUÉING THE DESIGNS

I used needle-turn appliqué to make all the projects because I like the more traditional look it creates. Use the appliqué method you're most comfortable with. If you choose to use fusible appliqué, follow the manufacturer's instructions, and please note that all nonsymmetrical appliqué images will need to be reversed when tracing.

1 Prepare the appliqué background by tracing the cutting line of the pattern onto the background fabric, leaving up to ½" of space around all sides to allow for fabric distortion and fraying while stitching. *Don't cut out the exact block size until you have completed all stitching.* For example, for the Ornaments block in "Christmas Story Quilt" on page 50, draw a 3½" x 8½" rectangle onto the background fabric and cut around the rectangle ½" beyond the drawn lines to get a 4½" x 9½" rectangle. Complete the appliqué and embroidery; then trim the rectangle to the exact 3½" x 8½" size.

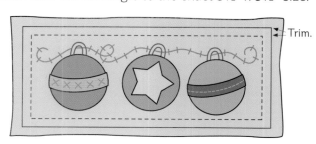

Trim.

2 Tape the pattern over a light source, such as a window or light box. Then position the appliqué background fabric over the pattern and tape in place. Use a soft pencil or water-soluble marker to lightly trace some key elements of the design to help with appliqué placement. Trace all parts of the design that are to be embroidered, such as words, stems, or stars, onto the appliqué background using a Pigma pen or pencil.

3 Trace each appliqué shape onto freezer paper to make a template. Do not add seam allowances to these shapes. Cut out the templates, iron them onto the right side of the appliqué fabric, then trace around each shape using a pencil or water-soluble marker. If you prefer, trace the shapes directly onto the appliqué fabrics using a light box.

4 Cut out each shape, adding a scant ¼" seam allowance to all sides.

5 Pin and stitch the appliqué shapes onto the background fabric using a thread that blends with the appliqué piece. Use the point and edge of your needle to turn the seam allowance under at the drawn line as you go. Slipstitch the appliqué

pieces into place. Clip curves to the drawn line to allow the appliqué fabric to turn smoothly. Sew the pieces that are overlapped first; for example, in the Xmas Treats appliqué in "Christmas Story Quilt", sew the candy canes before the pot.

6 Once the appliqués are complete, refer to the stitching guide to add the embroidery.

Appliqué Tip

For multiple appliqué shapes such as tongues and embroidered circles, make a template using heat-resistant template plastic. Trace around the template on the right side of the appliqué fabric with a pencil, then cut out the shape, leaving a seam allowance of about ¼". Place the template on the wrong side of the cutout shape and turn the seam allowance over the edge of the template, pressing it in place. A little bit of spray starch helps to hold it. Remove the template, and the appliqué is ready to be stitched into place.

SANTA'S SATCHEL

Every year my children are so excited to pull out their Santa bags to put under the tree on Christmas Eve. Even more exciting is waking up to see their bags full of surprises left by Santa the night before! Other possible uses? Consider using the tote as a reusable gift bag for a large item . . . hmmm, maybe even for a quilt.

FINISHED SIZE: 19" diameter x 28" tall

MATERIALS

Yardage is based on 42"-wide fabric, unless otherwise noted.

¼ yard *each* of 8 assorted prints for bag
6" x 13" rectangle of beige fabric for appliqué background
Assorted scraps (red, green, gold, brown, and blue) for appliqué
1 yard of fabric for lining
1 yard of Pellon lightweight fusible fleece
1½ yards of braided cord
6-strand embroidery floss in red, green, and brown

CUTTING

From *each* of the assorted prints, cut:
    3 squares, 5½" x 5½" (24 total)
    2 strips, 2½" x 20½" (16 total)
From *each of 2* of the prints, cut:
    1 circle using the pattern on page 29
From the lining fabric, cut:
    2 rectangles, 20½" x 31½"
From the fusible fleece, cut:
    2 rectangles, 20½" x 31½"
    1 circle

ASSEMBLING THE BAG

1 Appliqué the Christmas Tree on pattern sheet 2 onto the beige rectangle. Turn under the seam allowance and press. Set aside for now.

2 Sew four 5½" squares together in a row. Repeat to make a total of six strips, each measuring 5½" x 20½".

Make 6.

3 Sew one 2½" x 20½" strip of each color together along the long edge, creating a block measuring 16½" x 20½". This is the bag front. Repeat to make the bag back.

Make 2.

4 Sew a strip from step 2 to the top of the bag front. Sew two strips from step 2 to the bottom of the bag front. The bag front should now measure 20½" x 31½". Repeat to make the bag back.

5 Fuse fleece rectangles to the wrong side of the bag front and back. Fuse the fleece circle to one of the fabric circles.

6 Position the appliquéd rectangle on the bag front so that it's centered vertically and the top edge is 10¼" down from the top raw edge. Using a running stitch and two strands of red floss, stitch the appliqué in place.

7 With right sides facing, pin the bag front and back together along the sides. Sew 4¼" down from the top raw edge along one side and stop. Leave a 1" opening for the casing, then continue sewing the remainder of the side seam. Sew the other side seam without leaving an opening.

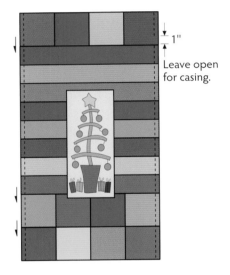

1"

Leave open for casing.

8 Using the longest stitch on your sewing machine, sew a gathering stitch around the lower edge of the bag, ¼" from the bottom raw edge. Fold the bag in half, then in half again, and mark each quarter with a pin. Repeat with one print circle.

9 With right sides together, match the pins of the bag to the pins of the circle. Gather the stitching from step 8, easing the bag to fit the circle. Pin in place, then stitch the circle to the bag using a ¼" seam allowance.

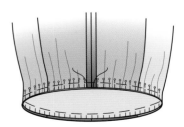

10 Repeat steps 7–9 using the lining fabric and the second fabric circle. Leave a 4" opening along one side seam for turning, but do not leave the 1" opening for the casing.

11 Place the pieced bag inside the bag lining with right sides together and seams matching. Stitch around the top edge, then turn right side out through the opening in the lining. Press the top seam flat, then topstitch along this seam, ¼" from the top of the bag.

12 To make a casing, stitch between the top row of squares and the first strip, stitching through both the main fabric and lining fabric. Stitch around the bag again 1" above the first line of stitching.

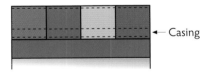

← Casing

13 Insert the cord by threading a safety pin through one end of the cord and feeding it through the casing at the open seam line. Tie the ends of the cord together.

TABLETOP TREE SKIRT

Spruce up your tabletop tree with an easy-to-embellish tree skirt that accessorizes it in style. Turn each tongue around the outer edge into an opportunity to sparkle by adding a fabric circle or a simple embroidery design. A little rickrack and a smattering of stars complete the look.

FINISHED SIZE: 29" diameter including tongues

MATERIALS

Yardage is based on 42"-wide fabric, unless otherwise noted.

1⅝ yards of red print for tree skirt and tongues
Assorted scraps for appliqués
¾ yard of lightweight fusible fleece
1⅝ yards of ⅜"-wide rickrack
¾ yard of ½"-wide ribbon
6-strand embroidery floss in the following colors: brown, cream, dark taupe, green, orange, and red
Heat-resistant template plastic or lightweight cardboard
Pencil and string
Large sheet of newspaper or other paper for pattern

CUTTING

From the red print, cut:
2 squares, 25" x 25"
From the fusible fleece, cut:
1 square, 25" x 25"

MAKING THE SKIRT

1 To make a paper template for the circle, tie one end of a piece of string around a pencil. Measure 12" from the pencil to the other end of the string. Pin the end of the string to the center of a large piece of newspaper, and hold the pencil at the other end so the string is taut. Draw a circle with the pencil, keeping the string taut as you move the pencil around. Cut out the paper template. This circle should have a 24" diameter.

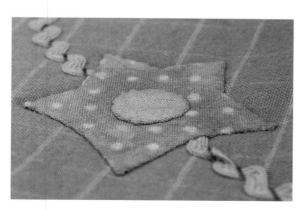

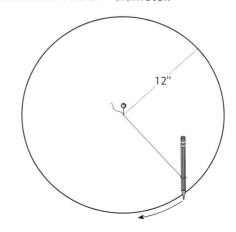

5 Make a tongue template from template plastic or cardboard using the pattern on pattern sheet 1. Fold the remaining red print in half with right sides together. Trace 24 tongues onto the wrong side of the fabric, leaving space between them for seam allowances. Sew on the drawn line of the tongues using a small machine stitch, leaving the straight edge open.

Fold

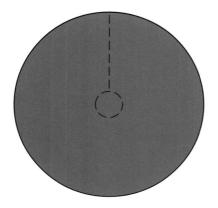

6 Cut the tongues apart and turn them right side out. Slide the template inside each tongue and press the tongue flat.

7 Make a plastic or cardboard template of the circle on the tongue pattern. Trace the circle onto scrap appliqué fabrics, cutting approximately ¼" outside the marked circles for seam allowance. I made 15 print circles and 9 tan solid circles that I embroidered. For embroidery circles, use any of the "Countdown to Christmas" designs on pattern sheet 2. Use two strands of floss and a backstitch to complete the embroidery. Position each circle on a tongue, referring to the pattern for placement. Turn under the edges and stitch in place.

8 Arrange the tongues around the outside of the tree skirt circle, face down and evenly spaced, with raw edges even with the edge of the circle. Pin and baste the tongues in place.

2 Fuse the fleece to the wrong side of one red-print square. Trace around the paper template onto the right side of the red-print square. Cut out the circle along the drawn line.

3 Trace and cut a second circle from the red print for the back of the tree skirt. Set this circle aside for now.

4 Use the circle pattern on page 29 to trace a small circle in the center of the large fabric circle. Cut from the outer edge of the large circle to the center of the circle, then cut out the small circle.

9 Baste a 12" length of ribbon to each side of the straight edge, 1" from the small circle and with raw edges even with the straight edge.

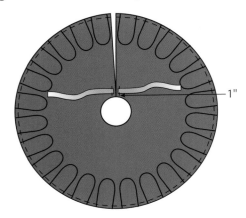

1"

Clip the seam allowance around the small circle to ensure everything will stay flat once turned. Turn right side out through the opening and press. Sew the opening closed.

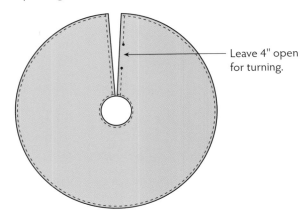

Leave 4" open for turning.

10 Place the tree-skirt top right sides together with the tree-skirt back, sandwiching the tongues and ribbons between the two layers. Pin the edges of the large circles together.

11 Sew the outside edge of the large circle, the two straight sides, and around the small circle, leaving a 4" opening along one straight side for turning. Cut the small circle and the side opening from the tree skirt back to match the top.

12 Referring to the photo below, pin rickrack to the circle, starting 3" from each straight edge and gently curving it around the outer edge. Sew in place using two strands of dark taupe floss.

13 Appliqué nine stars and circles over the rickrack using the Star Wreath pattern on pattern sheet 2.

14 Tie the skirt around the base of your tree and add lots of presents!

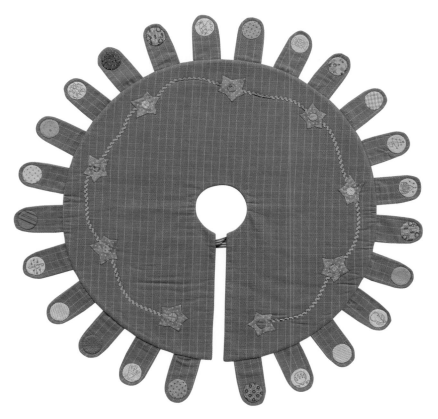

HE'S MAKING A LIST

You'll be checking twice to make sure your name ends up on the Nice side of this whimsical embroidered and appliquéd hanging. Personalize the handwritten tags for family or friends you'll be spending the holidays with, then watch to make sure your tag ends up on the right side come Christmas!

FINISHED SIZE: 5½" x 11"

MATERIALS

1 rectangle, 6" x 11½", of brown fabric for background
1 rectangle, 6" x 7", of cream print for appliqué background
1 rectangle, 6" x 7", of tan print for hill appliqué
Assorted scraps for appliqués
1 rectangle, 6" x 11½", of fabric for backing
1 rectangle, 6" x 11½", of lightweight fleece or batting
6-strand embroidery floss in the following colors: cream, dark taupe, and red
Two ½"-diameter (14 mm) buttons
Watercolor paint and paper
Single-hole punch
String for name tags

MAKING THE WALL HANGING

Patterns for the arched background and appliqués are on the pullout pattern sheets.

1 Make a paper pattern for the design by tracing the arch outline from the "First Day of Christmas" pattern and extending the length at the bottom by 1½". Inside the top of the arch, trace the left house, the Christmas tree, and the hill from the "Silent Night" pattern. Trace the "Naughty" and "Nice" block patterns from page 20, placing the bottom edge ¼" from the bottom of the outline. Trace the words "I've been really good this year . . . really" onto the hill. The paper template is now complete.

2 Using the paper template you've created, trace the arch outline onto the cream fabric.

3 Trace the appliqué shapes (tree, house, hill, and Naughty and Nice blocks) onto your chosen fabrics. For the hill, use the tan print. Trace the words and crosses onto the appliqué pieces. Pin the appliqué pieces onto the beige arch background and appliqué into place.

4 Stitch the words "I've been really good this year . . . . really" using a backstitch with two strands of dark taupe floss. Stitch the words "Naughty" and "Nice" using a backstitch with two strands of cream floss. Stitch two crosses in the sky using two strands of red floss.

5 Center the appliquéd and stitched piece on the 6" x 11½" brown background rectangle; pin. Appliqué it in place.

FINISHING THE WALL HANGING

1 Layer the fleece, the backing (right side up), and the appliquéd front (right side down) in that order. Sew around all sides ¼" in from the outer edge, leaving a 2" opening for turning. Clip the corners and turn right side out. Slipstitch the opening closed.

2 Quilt the wall hanging by stitching ¼" in from the outer edge using a running stitch and two strands of red floss.

3 Sew a button underneath the words Naughty and Nice.

4 Make some name tags to hang from the buttons using the pattern on page 20. Trace and cut the tags from watercolor paper and punch a hole at the top. Paint a watercolor wash on the tags to give them an aged look. Use the alphabet at right to add the names of family and friends or write them in your own hand. Tie string to the tags and hook over the buttons. Have fun moving the tags back and forth until Christmas Day!

ABCDEFGH
IJKLMNO
PQRSTUVW
XYZ
abcdefghijk
lmnopqrst
uvwxyz

I've been really good this year ....really ×××

Naughty Nice

He's Making a List block

Embroidery Key

- • French knot
- ×× Cross-stitch
- —— Backstitch

Patterns do not include seam allowances. Add seam allowance for needle-turn appliqué.

Name tag

PATCHWORK TABLE RUNNER

A handful of fabrics, a dash of patchwork, and a pinch of embroidery come together delightfully to create a hearty helping of cheer on a charming table runner. Rotate the miniature embroideries to suit your runner's location: turned in multiple directions for a great view no matter where you're seated, or facing one direction if your table is placed against a wall.

FINISHED SIZE: 12½" x 38", including tongues

MATERIALS

Yardage is based on 42"-wide fabric, unless otherwise noted. Fat eighths are 9" x 21" and fat sixteenths are 9" x 11".

1 fat eighth *each* of 7 dark prints

1 fat sixteenth *each* of 7 beige prints
½ yard of fabric for backing
½ yard of lightweight fleece
6-strand embroidery floss in the following colors: blue, brown, green, mustard, orange, and red
Heat-resistant template plastic or lightweight cardboard

CUTTING

From the dark-print fat eighths, cut a *total* of:
    27 squares, 3" x 3"*
    56 squares, 2⅛" x 2⅛"; cut in half diagonally to
      yield 112 triangles
    Assorted 1½"-wide strips measuring 2" to 5"
      in length, to make 4 strips that are *each*
      12½" long

From the beige-print fat sixteenths, cut a *total* of:
    28 squares, 2¼" x 2¼"

From the fleece, cut:
    1 rectangle, 12½" x 31½"

In the table runner shown, six of the dark squares were replaced by beige squares for added interest.

PIECING THE TABLE RUNNER

1 Sew dark-print triangles to opposite sides of a beige 2¼" square. Choose the triangles randomly. Press the seam allowances toward the triangles. Add triangles to the remaining two sides of the square, and press. Repeat for all 28 beige squares.

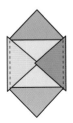

2 Join three units from step 1 and two dark-print 3" squares in a strip as shown. Repeat to make a total of six strips.

Make 6.

3 Join two units from step 1 and three dark-print 3" squares in a strip as shown. Repeat to make a total of five strips.

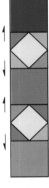

Make 5.

4 Arrange the strips in rows, alternating the strips from steps 2 and 3 as shown. Begin and end with strips from step 2. Sew the rows together.

5 Sew random 1½"-wide strips together end to end into four strips that measure 12½" long. Sew two strips to each end of the table runner.

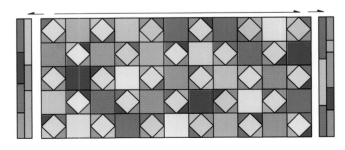

7 Stitch an assortment of embroidered circles using the "Countdown to Christmas" designs on pattern sheet 2. Use a backstitch with two strands of floss, using a single color for each design. Trace the circle around the design, cut out ¼" beyond the drawn line, and appliqué a circle to the end of each tongue. I made 13 circles in a variety of colors. Appliqué the remaining three circles randomly to some of the dark squares on the table runner.

8 Place five tongues face down on each end of the table runner. Position them so they are facing inward and are spaced evenly, with raw edges even with the edge of the table runner. Baste into position.

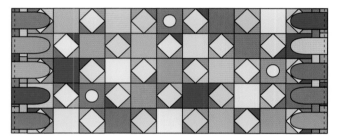

6 Make a tongue template using the pattern on pattern sheet 1. To make one tongue, fold a piece of dark fabric in half with right sides together. Trace the tongue onto the wrong side of the fabric, allowing room for a ¼" seam allowance. Sew on the drawn line of the tongue using a small machine stitch; leave the straight edge open. Turn the tongue right side out. Slide the template inside the tongue and press the tongue flat. Repeat to make 10 tongues.

9 Place the fleece, the backing (right side up), and the table runner (right side down) in that order. Make sure all the tongues are sandwiched between the table runner and the backing. Sew ¼" from the outer edge on all sides, leaving a 4" opening at one end for turning. Clip the corners and turn right side out. Slipstitch the opening closed.

10 Quilt the table runner. I hand quilted ¼" from all seam allowances on the large dark squares and small beige squares, and through the centers of the strips at each end of the table runner.

SMALL TREASURE TOTES

A jar of homemade jam, a bottle of infused olive oil, or a favorite wine—all great gifts or hostess thank-yous at the holidays. But how to make them a bit more personal? How about a handmade tote that doubles as a gift bag! Tall or small, make them ahead so you have several on hand. Then when the occasion arises, you'll be prepared!

SMALL TOTE BAG

FINISHED SIZE: 3½" diameter x 3¼" tall

MATERIALS

1 fat quarter (18" x 21") of red-and-green stripe for bag, lining, and handle
1 rectangle, 4" x 16", of lightweight fusible fleece
Assorted scraps for tongues and embroidered circles
6-strand embroidery floss in the following colors: blue, green, and red

CUTTING

The circle pattern is on page 29.

From the red-and-green stripe, cut:
  2 rectangles, 3¾" x 11½"
  1 rectangle, 2½" x 11½"
  2 circles
From the fusible fleece, cut:
  1 rectangle, 3¾" x 11½"
  1 circle

MAKING THE BAG

1 Following the manufacturer's instructions, iron the fusible fleece to the wrong side of one 3¾" x 11½" striped rectangle and one circle.

2 Using the small tongue pattern on page 27, trace and cut out five tongues and five small circles from scrap fabrics. Appliqué the tongues to the right side of the interfaced 3¾" x 11½" rectangle, beginning and ending ⅜" from the short edges and spacing them evenly.

3 Stitch three embroidery designs from the "Countdown to Christmas" designs on pattern sheet 2 onto three small circles using a backstitch and two strands of floss, then appliqué the circles to three of the tongues. Appliqué two plain fabric small circles to the remaining two tongues.

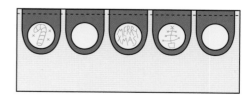

4 Fold the rectangle in half crosswise, right sides together, and sew the sides together.

5 Fold the rectangle in half, then in half again, and mark the four quarters with pins along the lower edge. Repeat for the interfaced circle.

6 With right sides together, match the pins on the bag to the pins on the circle. Pin in place, then stitch the circle to the bag using a ¼" seam allowance.

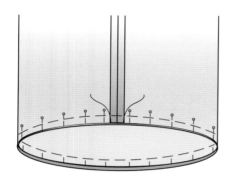

7 Repeat step 4 with the remaining 3¾" x 11½" rectangle, but leave a 2" opening in the seam for turning. Repeat steps 5 and 6 with this rectangle and the remaining circle. This is the lining; set aside for now.

8 To make the handle, fold the 2½" x 11½" rectangle in half lengthwise with right sides together. Sew the long raw edges together using a ¼" seam allowance. Turn right side out and press, centering the seam on one side. Topstitch along each long edge.

9 Pin the handle ends to the right side of the bag along the top edge. Make sure the ends are opposite each other and the raw edges are even with the top edge of the bag. Baste.

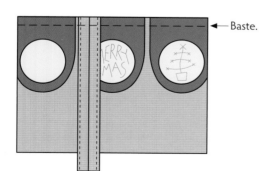

← Baste.

10 Nestle the main bag inside the bag lining with right sides together and the handle sandwiched in between. Stitch around the top edge, then turn right side out through the opening in the lining. Press the top seam flat. Stitch the opening in the lining closed.

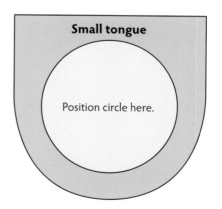

Small tongue

Position circle here.

Patterns do not include
seam allowances.
Add seam allowance
for needle-turn appliqué.

TALL TOTE BAG

FINISHED SIZE: 3½" diameter x 11" tall

MATERIALS

Yardage is based on 42"-wide fabric, unless otherwise noted.

½ yard of red-and-green stripe fabric for bag, lining, and handle

1 rectangle, 2½" x 11½", of coordinating fabric for appliqué strip

Assorted scraps of beige solid and color prints for appliqué circles

1 rectangle, 13" x 16", of lightweight fusible fleece

¼ yard of baby rickrack

6-strand embroidery floss in the following colors: dark taupe, green, orange, and red

CUTTING

From the red-and-green striped fabric, cut:
1 square, 11½" x 11½"
1 rectangle, 6½" x 11½"
1 rectangle, 3½" x 11½"
1 strip, 2½" x 11½"
2 circles using the pattern on page 29

From the fusible fleece, cut:
1 square, 11½" x 11½"
1 circle

MAKING THE BAG

1 Sew the 3½" x 11½" striped rectangle to one long edge of the 2½" x 11½" coordinating-fabric rectangle. Sew the 6½" x 11½" striped rectangle to the opposite long edge of the 2½" x 11½" rectangle. Press the seam allowances toward the striped rectangles.

2 Trace three embroidery designs from the "Countdown to Christmas" designs on pattern sheet 2 onto beige fabric and stitch them using a backstitch and two strands of floss. Cut out the embroidered circles. Using the same circle as a pattern, cut three print fabric circles for appliqués. Arrange the embroidered circles and plain fabric circles randomly along the strip, placing them at

different heights; appliqué in place. Sew the rickrack to the top of these ornaments. Be sure to start and end the rickrack at the same height so that the ends meet when the side seam is sewn. Sew the rickrack in place using two strands of dark taupe floss.

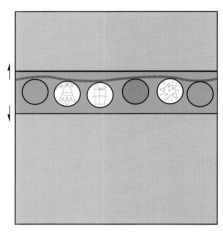

3 Following the manufacturer's instructions, fuse the 11½" x 11½" square of fleece to the wrong side of the pieced square, and the fleece circle to one fabric circle.

4 Fold the square in half crosswise, right sides together, and sew the side seam.

5 Fold the bag in half, then in half again, and mark the four quarters with pins along the lower edge. Repeat for the circle with the fleece.

6 With right sides together, match the pins on the bag to the pins on the circle. Pin in place, then stitch the circle to the bag using a ¼" seam allowance, referring to the illustration in step 6 on page 27.

7 Repeat step 4 with the remaining 11½" x 11½" square, but leave a 3" opening along the side seam for turning. Repeat steps 5 and 6 with this square and the remaining circle. This is the lining; set it aside for now.

8 To make the handle, fold the 2½" x 11½" handle strip in half lengthwise, right sides together. Sew the long raw edges together using a ¼" seam allowance. Turn right side out and press, centering the seam on one side. Topstitch along each side of the handle.

9 Pin the handle ends to the right side of the bag along the top edge. Make sure the ends are

opposite each other and the raw edges are even with top edge of the bag. Baste.

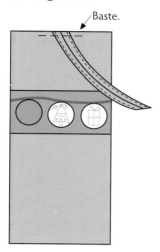

Baste.

10 Nestle the main bag inside the bag lining with right sides together and the handle sandwiched in between. Stitch along the top edge, then turn right side out through the opening in the lining. Press the top seam flat. Stitch the opening in the lining closed. Then insert the lining into the bag to complete.

**Circle for
Small Treasure Totes
Santa's Satchel
Tabletop Tree Skirt**

¼" seam allowance

COUNTDOWN TO CHRISTMAS

A clever wall hanging *does double duty* during the holidays, adding to your seasonal decor and serving as an anticipation builder. Used like an Advent calendar, it features 24 reversible ornaments—numbers on one side, holiday motifs on the opposite side—and a treetop star for Christmas Day! Need it do more? Tuck notes to Santa into the tree-base pocket.

FINISHED SIZE: 16½" x 28½"

MATERIALS

½ yard of tan print for background
⅓ yard of red print for border
⅛ yard of green print for tree
2 squares, 5" x 5", of brown fabric for pot
Assorted scraps for ornaments, star, and presents
⅓ yard of red-and-green print for binding
⅔ yard of fabric for backing
20" x 32" piece of batting
6-strand embroidery floss in the following colors:
    blue, brown, cream, green, medium teal,
    and red
24 buttons, ¼" (7 mm) each
Lightweight cardboard for ornaments
Template plastic (optional)
Pencil or water-soluble marker
Brown Pigma pen
Glue stick

CUTTING

From the tan print, cut:
    1 rectangle, 14½" x 26½"
From the red print, cut:
    2 strips, 2" x 13½"
    2 strips, 2" x 28½"
From the red-and-green print, cut:
    3 strips, 2½" x 42"
From the green print, cut:
    1 strip, ⅞" x 20"

APPLIQUÉING THE DESIGNS

All patterns are on pattern sheet 2.

1 Prepare the following appliqués: one *each* of presents #1 and #2, and five tree branches.

2 Turn under a ¼" seam allowance on all sides of the green ⅞" x 20" strip and press. Position this on the tan-print rectangle so that it's centered

vertically and the top is 1¾" down from the top edge. Appliqué in place.

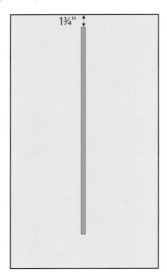

3 Trace the words and the pot detail in the center of one brown 5" square. Stitch the design using a backstitch with two strands of cream floss. When the stitching is completed, trace the pot outline onto the wrong side of the fabric, making sure the stitching is positioned correctly within the outline. Place a second square of pot fabric right sides together with the first square, and sew along the drawn pot outline leaving a 1¼" opening at the bottom of the pot for turning.

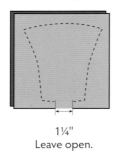

1¼"
Leave open.

4 Cut around the sewn line leaving a scant ¼" seam allowance. Trim the corners, turn the pot right side out, and press. It's not necessary to stitch the opening closed. Position the pot on the background fabric so that the bottom is 1¾" above the bottom edge. Appliqué the sides and bottom of the pot to the background, leaving the top open to form a pocket for Santa's letters.

5 Arrange the tree branches on the tree, referring to the dashed lines on the patterns to align

them with the tree trunk. Place the shortest one 2½" from the top of the trunk, the longest one 3" above the pot, and the remaining three at regular intervals along the trunk. Appliqué in place.

6 Appliqué presents #1 on the right side of the pot and presents #2 on the left side of the pot. Stitch the ribbons using two strands of floss in the following colors: blue, brown, green, medium teal, and red.

7 Trim the appliqué background to 13½" x 25½". Sew the 2" x 13½" border strips to the top and bottom of the block. Sew the 2" x 28½" border strips to the sides of the block. Press the seam allowances toward the border.

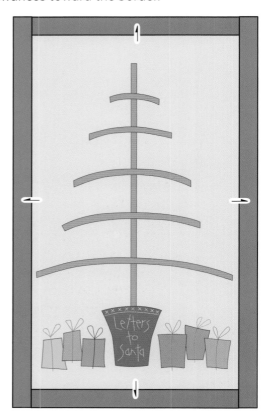

8 Refer to "Finishing the Quilt" on page 62 as needed to layer, baste, quilt, and bind the wall hanging. I quilted ¼" from all appliqués and seams, and quilted a few stars in the background using patterns from the Star Wreath on pattern sheet 2.

9 Sew a small button at each point marked with a dot on the branch patterns; these are for the ornaments to hang from.

MAKING THE ORNAMENTS AND STAR

I chose the ornament fabrics randomly, but each one is a fairly plain print. Use the same fabric for both the front and back of the ornament.

1 Using template plastic or cardboard, make a circle template by tracing one of the embroidery circle outlines on pattern sheet 2. Use this template to trace circles onto ornament fabrics and cardboard.

2 Trace a circle onto the desired ornament fabric using a pencil or water-soluble marker. Trace an embroidery design in the circle using a Pigma pen or white pencil. Stitch the design using a backstitch with two strands of cream floss. Cut out the circle, allowing a generous ¼" seam allowance beyond the drawn circle.

3 Repeat step 2 to create the back of the ornament, tracing and stitching a number from the patterns on pattern sheet 2.

4 Trace and cut out two cardboard circles. Center a stitched circle on a cardboard circle and use a glue stick to secure it. Glue the seam allowance to the back of the cardboard circle. Repeat with the second stitched circle.

5 Place a pin at the top of each circle and then place the two circles together with the images facing outward and the pins meeting. Whipstitch the edges of the circles together using thread that matches the fabric.

6 Make a hanging loop for the ornament by threading two strands of red floss into your needle. Insert the needle through the side of the sewn circle to the top of the ornament, sew a few stitches to secure the thread, then form a loop of the desired length (mine are all different lengths). Sew a few more stitches at the top of the ornament

to secure the thread once more, then take the needle through the circle and clip the thread back to the circle edge. Repeat steps 1–6 to make 24 ornaments total.

7 Using the same method as for the ornaments, make the star for the top of the tree using the pattern on the pullout pattern sheet. Trace and cut out two cardboard stars (one and one reversed) and two fabric stars (one and one reversed). Use two strands of red floss to stitch the crosses and words on one piece of star fabric. The reversed side of the star has no stitching. Glue the stars to the cardboard, then clip the fabric at the inner corners so the seam allowance will turn under smoothly. Make a small thread loop for the star—just enough so it can be swung around to read Xmas Day on December 25!

POCKETFUL OF WISHES

Good things come in small packages. That's especially true when the small package is handmade. Create this little pocket to hold your good wishes, tiny treasures, and more. If you make one for a stitching friend, she can use it to hold her needles and a skein of embroidery floss long after the holidays are over.

FINISHED SIZE: 3" x 4" when closed

MATERIALS

1 rectangle, 3½" x 8½", *each* of outer fabric and lining fabric

2 rectangles, 2½" x 2¾, of contrasting fabric for inner pocket

1 piece, 3½" x 8½", of lightweight fusible fleece

1 yard of ⅜"-wide ribbon

3" length of baby rickrack

6-strand embroidery floss in dark taupe and red

2" heart button or appliqué

MAKING THE POUCH

1 Pin a 3½" length of ribbon to the 3½" x 8½" outer fabric rectangle, positioning it 2" in from the edge. Attach the ribbon using a running stitch with two strands of red floss. Repeat on the other end.

2 Center the remaining ribbon along the length of the rectangle with the ribbon extending about 6" beyond the end of the fabric on each end. Sew using a running stitch as in step 1, starting and finishing ½" from the edge of the fabric. Set aside for now.

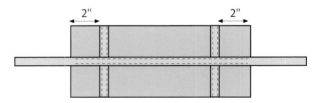

3 Pin the rickrack ½" down from the top raw edge of the 2½" x 2¾" inner-pocket fabric. Sew in place using two strands of dark taupe floss. Trace the words "Little presents are the best" below the sewn rickrack, and stitch using a backstitch and two strands of dark taupe floss.

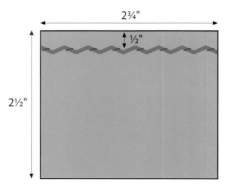

with all my love...

Little Presents are the best!

live your dream

4 Place the second 2½" x 2¾" inner-pocket rectangle over the first with right sides together. Sew around all sides, leaving a 1" opening along the bottom edge for turning. Turn right side out and press. Position the pocket on the 3½" x 8½" lining rectangle so it's centered vertically and the bottom edge is ⅝" from the bottom raw edge of the lining. Refer to the pattern on page 37 for placement. Slipstitch the pocket in place, leaving the top of the pocket open.

5 Trace the words "with all my love . . ." and the crosses onto the lining fabric. Using two strands of floss, stitch the words in dark taupe floss and the crosses in red floss. Sew a heart button beside the stitched words. If you prefer, appliqué the heart using the shape on the pattern.

6 Layer the fleece, the lining (right side up), and the outer fabric (right side down) in that order, making sure the ribbon is sandwiched between the layers. Sew ¼" from the outer edges, leaving a 2" opening for turning. Clip the corners and turn right side out; slipstitch the opening closed.

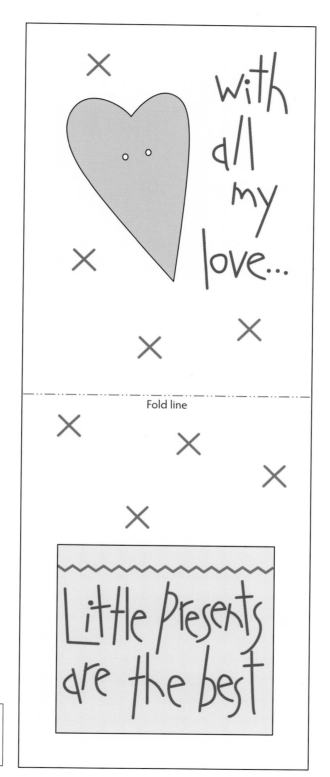

with all my love...

Fold line

Little presents are the best

Embroidery Key

● French knot

✕✕ Cross-stitch

—— Backstitch

Patterns do not include
seam allowances.
Add seam allowance to heart
for needle-turn appliqué.

Pocketful of Wishes pouch

PUNCHNEEDLE ORNAMENTS

I love the vintage look of these mini ornaments. Choose from 24 adorable motifs that represent some of my favorite holiday things. Add a simple blanket-stitched backing and you've got a stunning set of ornaments you'll treasure for generations! Or tie a single ornament to a package for a dear friend and watch as her eyes light up. "You made it for me?"

FINISHED SIZE: 2" diameter

MATERIALS FOR 1 ORNAMENT

1 square, 6" x 6", of weavers cloth or other tightly woven fabric

1 rectangle, 2½" x 5", of felt for backing

6-strand embroidery floss in the following colors: brown, caramel, dark coffee, dark taupe, ecru, gray, green, medium teal, mustard, orange, red, and yellow

Punchneedle tool

Brown Pigma pen

6" embroidery hoop

MAKING THE ORNAMENT

1 Using a light source, trace any of the "Countdown to Christmas" embroidery circles on pattern sheet 2 onto weavers cloth using a Pigma pen. Place the traced fabric in a hoop and pull taut.

2 Stitch the designs using three strands of embroidery floss in the colors listed in the Stitching Guide on page 40. Set the punchneedle tool on the smallest setting (#1) and refer to the manufacturer's instructions as needed. If you're punching and no loops are forming, check to make sure you haven't caught the end of the thread, as it must remain free at all times.

Punchneedle Ornaments
Stitching Guide

Outline the image first, then fill it in.

Gingerbread Man
Body: dark coffee
Eyes, mouth, buttons: dark taupe
Arm and leg detail: ecru
Background: gray

Pear
Pear: mustard and dark coffee together
Leaves: green
Stalk and leaf detail: dark coffee
Background: dark taupe

Christmas Tree
Pot: dark coffee
Tree: green
Star on tree top: mustard
Stars on branches: orange
Background: gray

Star
Star: mustard
Crosses: red
Rays: green
Background: gray

Stocking
Top, toe, and heel: orange
Stocking: green
Crosses: yellow
String: dark coffee
Background: gray

Heart
Heart: medium teal
Spots: orange
Background: dark taupe

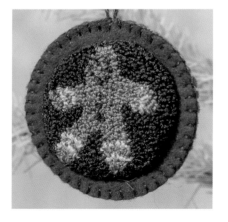

3 When you've finished punching, use your needle to move any loops to sharpen distorted lines. Clip loose ends on the front of the design even with the height of the loops.

4 Place the design face down on an ironing surface and gently steam press. Place the design on a fluffy towel to help keep the loops from being pressed flat. Cut out the design ½" from the worked edge. Turn the seam allowance under and press into position with a hot iron.

5 Cut two circles of felt using the punchneedle ornament pattern, below. Center the punchneedle work on one of the felt circles and slipstitch into place using a matching thread.

6 To make a hanging loop, cut a 20" length of red floss. Holding three strands together, twist them until the loop starts to twist back on itself. Tie the two ends together so the loop is about 3¾" long.

7 Place the second felt circle on the back of the first and stitch them together using two strands of dark taupe floss and a blanket stitch. When you reach the top of the circle, insert the hanging loop between the felt circles, hiding the knot, and stitch the opening closed.

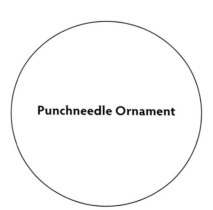

Punchneedle Ornament

12 DAYS OF CHRISTMAS

End the debate over whether it's 9 ladies dancing and 10 lords a-leaping or the other way around. Whip up this skinny stitchery using a simple backstitch and you'll have a visual reminder of all the verses of this perennial favorite holiday song. It's so sweet and simple. Trace, stitch, and enjoy!

FINISHED SIZE: 5¾" x 36½"

MATERIALS

Yardage is based on 42"-wide fabric, unless otherwise noted.

¼ yard of cream fabric for embroidery background
½ yard of green print for background and backing, cut into two pieces, each 8" x 42"
¼ yard of lightweight fleece
6-strand embroidery floss in the following colors: blanc, blue, brown, caramel, dark coffee, dark taupe, dusky rose, green, medium teal, orange, red, and yellow
2 heart buttons, approximately 1" tall
Fine-point Pigma pen

STITCHING THE DESIGN

1 Using the patterns on pages 46–49, trace the designs in order onto one piece of tracing paper to make a complete pattern; do not leave space between the sections. Tape the pattern in place over a light source such as a window or light box. Then tape the cream fabric, right side up, over the pattern and trace the design onto the fabric using a fine-point Pigma pen.

2 Stitch the design using two strands of floss unless otherwise indicated. Refer to the Stitching Guide on page 44 for colors. Use a backstitch throughout except where noted.

FINISHING THE WALL HANGING

1 When the stitching is complete, trim the cream rectangle to 1" beyond the stitched brown border on all sides. Turn the cream fabric under ¼" beyond the stitching and press. Center the stitched design on a green print rectangle and appliqué in place.

2 Trim the green background 1" beyond the cream applique on all sides. This should measure 6¼" x 37". Cut the backing and the fleece to the same size.

3 Layer the fleece, backing (right side up), and appliquéd front (right side down) in that order. Sew ¼" in from the outer edge on all sides, leaving a 2" opening for turning. Clip the corners and turn right side out. Slipstitch the opening closed.

4 Quilt by stitching ¼" from the outer edge and the appliqué using a running stitch with two strands of caramel floss. Attach the heart buttons to the top corners.

Partridge in a pear tree

♡ 2 Turtle Doves ♡ x

3 French Hens

4 Calling Birds

x 5 Golden rings ♡ x x x

6 Geese-a-laying

7 Swans-a-swimming

12 Days of Christmas Stitching Guide

For all designs:
Borders, words (bs), eyes (fk): brown

Partridge in a Pear Tree:
Body: red
Beak: yellow
Legs: brown
Pear: green

2 Turtle Doves:
Hearts: dusky rose
Bodies: medium teal
Beaks: orange
Star: yellow

3 French Hens
Snail, tower: 1 strand of dark coffee
Scarves, berets: red
Garland: green
Berries: orange
Beaks, feet: yellow
Bodies: blanc

4 Calling Birds
Wire: dark coffee
Music notes: caramel
Beaks, legs: orange
Bodies: blue

5 Golden Rings
Hearts: red
Vine: green
String holding hearts: 1 strand of brown
Rings: yellow

6 Geese a-Laying
Beaks, legs: dark coffee
Bodies: caramel
Eggs: blanc

7 Swans a-Swimming
Boat: dark coffee
Rings: red
Sail: caramel
Water: medium teal
Beaks: orange
Crosses: blue
Bodies: blanc

8 Maids a-Milking
Cow: dark coffee
Dresses, mouths: 1 strand of dusky rose
Cow udder/horns; maids' faces, arms, legs: 1 strand of caramel
Buckets: brown
Boots: dark taupe
Milk lid, words: 1 strand of blue
Hair: 1 strand of yellow
Milk bottle: blanc

9 Ladies Dancing
Shoes, hats: 1 strand of dark coffee
Flowers: 1 strand of red
Lips: 1 strand of dusky rose
Faces, arms, legs: 1 strand of caramel
Dresses: medium teal
Tree, flower stems: green
Dress detail: orange
Star on tree: yellow

10 Lords a-Leaping
Tree: dark coffee
Star on tree: red
Mouths: dusky rose
Faces: 1 strand of caramel
Tops: green
Pants: brown
Crowns: orange
Shoes: dark taupe

11 Pipers Piping
Pants: dark coffee
Star on tree: red
Music notes, faces: 1 strand of caramel
Tree: green
Pot, hair: 1 strand of brown
Shoes: dark taupe
Tops: blue
Trumpets: yellow

12 Drummers Drumming
Drums: dark coffee
Tops: red
Faces: 1 strand of caramel
Pants, shoes, hats: dark taupe

8 Maids-a-milking

9 Ladies dancing

10 Lords a-leaping

11 Pipers Piping

12 Drummers drumming

Join to 6 Geese a-Laying on page 47.

**12 Days of Christmas
embroidery pattern**

Embroidery Key

● French knot

✕✕ Cross-stitch

—— Backstitch

Join to 5 Golden Rings on page 46.

6 Geese a-laying

7 Swans a-swimming

8 Maids a-milking

Join to 9 Ladies Dancing on page 48.

Join to 8 Maids a-Milking on page 47.

9 Ladies dancing

10 Lords a-leaping

**12 Days of Christmas
embroidery pattern**

Embroidery Key

● French knot

✕✕ Cross-stitch

— Backstitch

Join to 11 Pipers Piping on page 49.

Join to 10 Lords a-Leaping on page 48.

11 Pipers Piping

12 Drummers drumming

CHRISTMAS STORY QUILT

Whether it is the tree and all the trimmings, the sweets and the traditions, or the gathering of friends and family—the joys of the holiday season make their appearance here. Worked in five blocks with a little stitchery and a bit of appliqué, you'll have a jolly time bringing all the elements together into a quilt you can treasure year after year.

FINISHED SIZE: 37½" x 42½"

BEFORE YOU BEGIN

The quilt is assembled block by block, with cutting instructions included at the beginning of each block, and border and finishing instructions included at the end of the project. Refer to the quilt photo for help with color placement. All appliqué patterns are on the pullout pattern sheets.

MATERIALS

Yardage is based on 42"-wide fabric unless otherwise noted. Fat quarters are 18" x 21".

⅜ yard *each* of 6 beige prints and 1 blue for backgrounds and border
1 fat quarter *each* of 16 assorted medium and dark prints for appliqué and piecing*
¼ yard of blue print for inner border
3" x 7" scrap of dark green for Christmas tree in Silent Night block
Small scrap of cream for angels' faces
7" x 7" scrap of burgundy wool for berries in Candle Holder and Star Wreath blocks
½ yard of tan print for binding
1⅜ yards of fabric for backing**
45" x 50" piece of batting

6-strand embroidery floss in the following colors: blue, brown, caramel, dark coffee, dark taupe, dusky rose, green, light brown, medium teal, orange, red, and yellow

*I used the following fabrics: two brown, two medium green, two red tone on tone, one medium blue/gray, one blue check, one teal stripe, one teal floral, one red dot, one red check, one burnt orange, one light-mustard check, one dark mustard, and one dark teal.

**If your fabric is not at least 42" wide after removing the selvages, you will need 2½ yards.

STAR BLOCK

There are five star blocks in this quilt. I used a different color for each star and background.

CUTTING FOR 1 BLOCK

From a beige print, cut:
4 squares, 1½" x 1½"
2 rectangles, 1½" x 2½"
From the assorted medium and dark prints, cut:
2 squares, 1½" x 1½"
1 rectangle, 1½" x 3½"

Star block

MAKING THE BLOCK

1 Place a 1½" medium or dark print square on one end of a 1½" x 2½" beige rectangle, right sides together. Sew diagonally across the square as shown. Trim the excess fabric from the corner, leaving ¼" seam allowances, and press the triangle toward the corner. Make two.

2 Sew a 1½" beige square to the end of each unit from step 1 as shown.

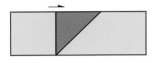

Make 2.

3 Place a 1½" beige square on one end of a 1½" x 3½" print rectangle. Sew diagonally across the background square as shown. Trim the excess fabric from the corner, leaving ¼" seam allowances, and press the triangle toward the corner. Position and sew a beige square on the other end of the rectangle, placing it on the opposite corner as shown.

4 Sew the units from steps 2 and 3 together to complete the Star block. The block should measure 3½" x 3½". Repeat to make a total of five Star blocks.

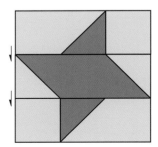

BLOCK A

CUTTING

From the assorted medium and dark prints, cut:
1 rectangle, 7½" x 11½", for First Day of Christmas background
10 squares, 1½" x 1½"
1 square, 2½" x 2½"
1 rectangle, 1½" x 6½"
1 rectangle, 1½" x 5½"
2 rectangles, 1½" x 8½", and 2 rectangles, 1½" x 5½", from the same fabric

From the assorted beige prints, cut:
1 rectangle, 9½" x 11½", for Singing Angels
1 rectangle, 4½" x 9½", for Ornaments

From the blue print for background, cut:
1 square, 6½" x 6½", for Candle Holder

APPLIQUÉING THE DESIGNS

1 Prepare the following appliqués. Cut the berries from the burgundy wool; do not add a seam allowance.

- **First Day of Christmas:** 1 arch, 1 bird, 1 wing, 1 pear
- **Singing Angels:** 3 halos, 3 faces, 3 books, 3 skirts, 1 underskirt, 6 wings, 6 shoes
- **Ornaments:** 3 ornaments, 1 star, 2 contrasting strips on ornaments
- **Candle Holder:** 1 candle, 1 flame, 1 candle holder, 1 handle, 16 berries

2 Appliqué the pieces to the background fabrics. Refer to the "Block A Stitching Guide" on page 54 to add embroidery to the appliquéd blocks.

3 After all stitching is complete, trim the backgrounds to the following sizes: First Day of Christmas, 6½" x 10½"; Singing Angels, 8½" x 10½"; Ornaments, 3½" x 8½"; Candle Holder, 5½" x 5½".

Block A

ASSEMBLING BLOCK A

1 Sew eight 1½" squares together in a row. Sew the two remaining 1½" squares together, then add them to one end of the 1½" x 6½" rectangle as shown. Press all seam allowances as shown.

2 Sew the units from step 1 together as shown, taking care to orient them correctly, then sew the 2½" square to the end of the unit. Press the seam allowances toward the square.

3 Join the unit from step 2 to the bottom of the Singing Angels appliqué; then sew this to the right edge of the First Day of Christmas appliqué. Press the seam allowances toward the appliqué pieces as you join them.

4 Sew the 1½" x 8½" rectangles to the top and bottom of the Ornaments appliqué. Sew a 1½" x 5½" rectangle to each short side of the appliqué. Sew a 1½" x 5½" rectangle to the right edge of the Candle Holder appliqué, then sew this to the right edge of the Ornament unit. Press the seam allowances as shown.

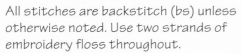

5 Sew the unit from step 4 to the bottom of the unit from step 3. The completed block should measure 15½" x 16½".

Block A
Stitching Guide

All stitches are backstitch (bs) unless otherwise noted. Use two strands of embroidery floss throughout.

First Day of Christmas
Outer circle on bird's eye: caramel
Words: brown
Stars, inner circle on bird's eye, beak (ss): mustard
Legs, center of eye (fk): dark taupe

Singing Angels
First angel's hair bows and earring detail (fk): red
Angel mouths: dusky rose
Words, heels, book spines, hair on first and third angels: brown
Legs, earring chains: light brown
Hair on center angel, writing on books, eyes (fk): dark taupe

Ornaments
Tinsel: green
Ornament details: mustard
Ornament loops: dark taupe

Candle Holder
Candle wick: caramel
Berry stems: dark taupe

BLOCK B

CUTTING

From the assorted medium and dark prints, cut:
    11 squares, 1½" x 1½"
    6 squares, 2½" x 2½"
    3 rectangles, 1½" x 3½"
    1 rectangle, 1½" x 4½"
From the assorted beige prints, cut:
    1 rectangle, 7½" x 9½", for Hang the Stockings
    1 rectangle, 7½" x 12½", for Christmas Wish Angel

APPLIQUÉING THE DESIGNS

1 Prepare the following appliqués:
   • **Hang the Stockings:** 4 stockings, 4 cuffs
   • **Christmas Wish Angel:** 1 dress, 2 sleeves, 2 hands, 1 face, 2 shoes, 1 hair, 1 halo, 1 bag, 1 bag trim

2 Appliqué the pieces to the background fabrics. Refer to the "Block B Stitching Guide" on page 55 to add embroidery to the appliquéd blocks.

Block B

3 After all stitching is complete, trim the backgrounds to the following sizes: Hang the Stockings, 6½" x 8½"; Christmas Wish Angel, 6½" x 11½.

ASSEMBLING BLOCK B

1 Sew two Star blocks together, pressing the seam allowances toward the bottom block; then sew the joined blocks to the left edge of the Hang the Stockings appliqué. Press the seam allowances toward the appliqué.

2 Join six 1½" squares in a row; press the seam allowances as shown. Sew the unit to the left of the stars as shown, pressing the seam allowances toward the stars. Sew six 2½" squares in a row; press the seam allowances in one direction as shown, then sew the row to the bottom of the unit.

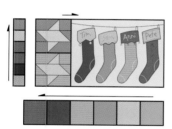

3 Sew two 1½" squares to one end of the 1½" x 4½" rectangle; press the seam allowances in one direction. Sew this unit to the left side of the Christmas Wish Angel appliqué, taking care to orient it correctly. Press the seam allowances toward the appliqué.

4 Sew the three 1½" x 3½" rectangles together end to end; then sew the remaining three 1½" squares to one end of this strip. Press the seam allowances toward the squares. Join the completed strip to the bottom of the unit from step 3.

5 Sew the unit from step 4 to the bottom of the unit from step 2 to complete block B. The block should measure 12½" x 15½".

Block B
Stitching Guide

All stitches are backstitch (bs) unless otherwise noted. Use two strands of embroidery floss throughout. Trace letters for names from the alphabet on the pullout pattern sheet.

Hang the Stockings
Bell outline on first stocking, dots on second stocking cuff (fk), detail on fourth stocking cuff (rs): red
Toes and heels (rs), name on third stocking: caramel
String holding stockings, hanging loops, name on second stocking: brown

Crosses on third stocking (cs), center of bells on first stocking (ss): orange
Names on first and fourth stockings, crosses on fourth stocking (cs): dark taupe

Christmas Wish Angel
Lips: dusky rose
Words on bag: caramel
Bag handle, heels on shoes: brown
Legs: light brown
Crosses (cs) and stars: mustard
Eyes (fk): dark taupe

BLOCK C

CUTTING

From the assorted medium and dark prints, cut:
- 30 squares, 1½" x 1½"
- 7 squares, 2½" x 2½"
- 6 rectangles, 1½" x 2½"
- 4 rectangles, 1½" x 3½"
- 1 rectangle, 1½" x 4½"
- 2 rectangles, 1½" x 6½"

From the assorted beige prints, cut:
- 1 rectangle, 7½" x 8½", for Presents
- 1 rectangle, 5½" x 7½", for Pudding
- 1 rectangle, 7½" x 9½", for Christmas Treats

APPLIQUÉING THE DESIGNS

1 Prepare the following appliqués:
- **Presents:** 3 presents, 3 labels, 3 ribbon bows, 3 ribbon lengths, 2 ribbon widths
- **Pudding:** 3 berries, 2 leaves, 1 icing, 1 pudding
- **Christmas Treats:** 1 pot, 1 star, 3 lollipops, 2 candy canes, 1 gingerbread man

2 Appliqué the pieces to the background fabrics. Refer to the "Block C Stitching Guide" on page 57 to add embroidery to the appliquéd blocks.

3 After all stitching is complete, trim the backgrounds to the following sizes: Presents, 6½" x 7½"; Pudding, 4½" x 6½"; Christmas Treats, 6½" x 8½".

ASSEMBLING BLOCK C

1 Sew two Star blocks together; press the seam allowances to one side. Join three 1½" squares in a row; press the seam allowances as shown, and then sew this row to one side of the star block row. Sew the completed unit to the bottom of the Presents appliqué. Press the seam allowances toward the appliqué.

2 Sew two 1½" x 3½" rectangles together end to end. Add a 1½" square to one end. Press the seam allowances to one side. Sew the completed strip to the top of the Presents appliqué as shown. Press the seam allowances away from the appliqué.

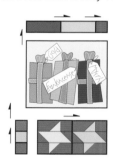

Block C

Block C
Stitching Guide

All stitches are backstitch (bs) unless otherwise noted. Use two strands of embroidery floss throughout.

Presents
Ribbon detail (rs): caramel
Words and hole on tags: brown
String: dark taupe

Pudding
Icing detail (rs): dark coffee

Christmas Treats
Leg and arm detail on gingerbread man (bs, rs): caramel
Lines on pot: medium teal
Words and stems: brown
Crosses (cs): mustard
Lollipop detail: orange
Eyes, mouth, buttons on gingerbread man (fk): dark taupe

3 Sew eight 1½" squares together in pairs and then join the pairs to make two four-patch units. Join the two four-patch units and three 2½" squares as shown, pressing the seam allowances in one direction. Sew the completed unit to the right edge of the Presents appliqué.

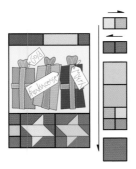

4 Sew four 1½" squares together end to end. Press the seam allowances in one direction. Add the 1½" x 4½" rectangle to one side. Add a 2½" square to the top as shown, then sew the completed unit to the right edge of the Pudding appliqué. Add a 1½" x 6½" rectangle to the opposite edge of the

Pudding appliqué. Press the seam allowances toward the appliqué.

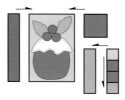

5 Sew two 1½" squares together. Join these squares with three 2½" squares, pressing the seam allowances as shown, and add the completed unit to the bottom of the Pudding appliqué.

6 Sew two 1½" squares to each end of a 1½" x 3½" rectangle, pressing the seam allowances as shown. Sew one 1½" square to the end of a 1½" x 6½" rectangle. Press the seam allowances toward the rectangle. Add these two units to the top of the Pudding appliqué.

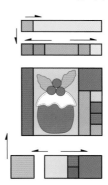

7 Sew two 1½" x 2½" rectangles together end to end; add two 1½" squares to one end. Press the seam allowances in one direction. Sew the completed unit to the bottom of the Christmas Treats appliqué.

8 Sew a 1½" x 2½" rectangle to opposite sides of a 1½" square. Add a 1½" square to one end; press the seam allowances in one direction, and then join the completed unit to the top of the Christmas Treats appliqué as shown on page 58.

9 Sew a 1½" x 2½" rectangle and a 1½" x 3½" rectangle end to end. Add two 1½" squares to one end, and a 1½" square and a 1½" x 2½" rectangle to the other end. Press the seam

allowances as shown. Sew the completed unit to the right edge of the Christmas Treats appliqué.

10 Join the three completed block sections and press the seam allowances as shown. Appliqué four fabric circles to the left of the Pudding appliqué using a berry from the Pudding appliqué as a template. The completed block should measure 10½" x 23½".

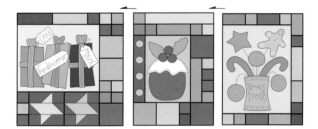

BLOCK D

CUTTING

From the assorted medium and dark prints, cut:
   10 squares, 1½" x 1½"
   6 squares, 2½" x 2½"
   2 rectangles, 1½" x 2½"
   3 rectangles, 1½" x 3½"
   1 rectangle, 1½" x 4½"

From the assorted beige prints, cut:
   1 rectangle, 7½" x 11½", for Silent Night

From the teal floral or another medium or dark print, cut:
   1 square, 9½" x 9½", for Star Wreath

APPLIQUÉING THE DESIGNS

1 Prepare the following appliqués. Cut the berries from the burgundy wool; do not add seam allowance.

   - **Star Wreath:** 1 circle background, 5 stars, 5 star centers, 15 berries
   - **Silent Night:** 3 doors, 7 windows, 3 walls, 3 roofs, 3 chimneys, 2 stars, 1 hill, 1 tree trunk, 4 branches

2 Appliqué the pieces to the background fabrics. Refer to the "Block D Stitching Guide" on page 59 to add embroidery to the appliquéd blocks.

3 After all stitching is complete, trim the backgrounds to the following sizes: Star Wreath, 8½" x 8½"; Silent Night, 6½" x 10½".

Block D

ASSEMBLING BLOCK D

1 Sew four 1½" squares together in a row. Sew two 2½" squares together, and join the two units as shown. Press all seam allowances as shown.

2 Sew a 1½" square to the end of a 1½" x 2½" rectangle. Press the seam allowances toward the square. Sew this unit to a Star block as shown below. Sew this unit to the bottom of the unit from step 1, and sew the completed section to the right edge of the Star Wreath appliqué. Press the seam allowances toward the appliqué.

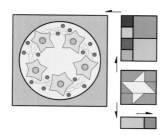

3 Sew three 1½" x 3½" rectangles end to end and add a 1½" square to one end. Press the seam allowances in one direction. Add the completed unit to the top of the Silent Night appliqué.

4 Sew four 1½" squares together in a row. Add a 1½" x 4½" rectangle to one end and a 1½" x 2½" rectangle to the opposite end. Press the seam allowances in one direction. Sew the completed unit to the bottom of the Silent Night appliqué.

5 Sew four 2½" squares together in a row; press the seam allowances in one direction. Add the row to the right edge of the Silent Night appliqué.

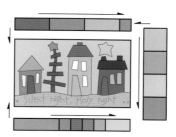

6 Sew the Star Wreath section to the left edge of the Silent Night section. The completed block should measure 8½" x 23½".

BLOCK E

CUTTING

From the assorted medium and dark prints, cut:
    5 squares, 1½" x 1½"
    2 rectangles, 1½" x 3½" and 2 rectangles,
        1½" x 5½", from the same fabric
From the assorted beige prints, cut:
    1 rectangle, 6½" x 13½", for Christmas Tree
From the blue print, cut:
    1 square, 4½" x 4½", for Humbug

APPLIQUÉING THE DESIGNS

1 Prepare the following appliqués:
  • **Humbug:** 1 background circle, 1 body, 1 head
  • **Christmas Tree:** 1 tree trunk, 4 branches, 1 star, 8 ornaments, 1 pot, 4 presents

2 Appliqué the pieces to the background fabrics. Refer to the "Block E Stitching Guide" on page 60 to add embroidery to the appliquéd blocks.

3 After all stitching is complete, trim the backgrounds to the following sizes: Humbug, 3½" x 3½"; Christmas Tree, 5½" x 12½".

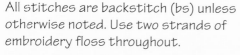

Block D Stitching Guide

All stitches are backstitch (bs) unless otherwise noted. Use two strands of embroidery floss throughout.

Star Wreath
Detail on star centers (rs): *red*
Stems: *green*
Berries (bus): *orange*

Silent Night
Words: *dark taupe*

Block E

ASSEMBLING BLOCK E

1 Sew the 1½" x 3½" rectangles to the top and bottom of the Humbug appliqué, and sew the 1½" x 5½" rectangles to the sides. Press the seam allowances toward the rectangles.

2 Sew five 1½" squares together in a row, press the seam allowances in one direction, and add the row to the bottom of the unit from step 1.

3 Sew the unit from step 2 to the bottom edge of the Christmas Tree appliqué to complete the block. The block should measure 5½" x 18½".

CUTTING FOR BORDERS AND BINDING

From the blue print, cut:
  4 strips, 1" x 42"
From the assorted beige prints, cut:
  4½"-wide strips in random lengths from 7" to 12", to equal a total of 154"
From the tan print, cut:
  4 strips, 2½" x 42"

ASSEMBLING THE QUILT TOP

1 Referring to the quilt diagram on page 61, sew block A to block B, and sew block C to block D. You may need to re-press some seam allowances so they nestle together neatly.

2 Join block E to the right edge of the C/D unit. Sew the C/D/E unit to the bottom edge of the A/B unit.

3 Measure the width of the quilt top through the center and cut two blue inner-border strips to the measured length. Sew the strips to the top and bottom of the quilt top. Press the seam allowances toward the border.

4 Measure the length of the quilt top through the center, including the top and bottom borders. Cut two blue inner-border strips to the measured length and sew them to the sides of the quilt top. Press the seam allowances toward the border.

5 Randomly sew the 4½"-wide strips of beige fabrics end to end. In the same manner as for the inner border, measure the width of the quilt top through the center and cut two border strips to the measured length.

6 Prepare 40 tongues for appliqué using the pattern on pattern sheet 1. Beginning 1¼" in from each end, arrange 9 tongues on each border strip, spacing them evenly; appliqué in place. Stitch

several embroidery designs from pattern sheet 2 onto scraps of beige fabrics. Trace the circles around the designs, cut out the circles ¼" beyond the drawn lines, and appliqué the circles randomly onto some of the tongues. Sew the appliquéd borders to the top and bottom of the quilt top.

7 Measure the length of the quilt top through the center, including the top and bottom borders. Cut two border strips to the measured length. Appliqué 11 tongues to each strip, this time beginning 5¼" in from each end. Add embroidered circles to some of the tongues. Sew the appliquéd strips to the sides of the quilt top.

Quilt layout

FINISHING THE QUILT

1 Cut the backing and batting about 4" larger than the quilt top.

2 Lay the backing (right side down), batting, and pressed quilt top (right side up) in that order. Make sure everything is flat and smooth.

3 Baste the three layers together before quilting. Begin basting in the center and work your way out to the edges going vertically, horizontally, and diagonally. Add extra basting lines to hold the three layers together more securely around the outer edges of the quilt. Alternatively, pin the three layers together using safety pins.

4 Quilt as desired. I primarily quilted around each appliqué shape, including the tongues, and quilted Xs through the plain square in the setting. Trim excess batting and backing to the edge of the quilt top.

5 Join the 2½"-wide cream-print strips end to end to make one long strip. Press the seam allowances open. Trim one end of the strip at a 45° angle. Turn under ¼" and press. Press the strip in half lengthwise with wrong sides together.

Fold line

6 Beginning in the center of one edge, pin the binding to the quilt top with raw edges even. Sew along one side at a time, using a ¼" seam allowance and stitching through all layers. Stop stitching ¼" from the corner and remove from the machine.

7 Fold the binding at a 90° angle away from the quilt top, then bring it straight down over itself in line with the next raw edge to be sewn. Stitch the second side. Repeat for each corner.

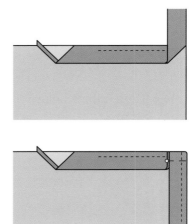

8 Stop stitching 6" before the starting point and remove the quilt from the machine. Lay the end of the binding over the beginning and trim the end at an angle so it overlaps the beginning by ½" to 1½". Tuck the end inside the fold of the beginning and finish stitching the binding to the quilt.

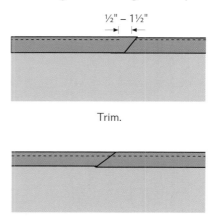

½" – 1½"

Trim.

9 Turn the folded edge of the binding over to the back and hand stitch along the previous sewing line, mitering the corners as you go.